Harald Bachner

Clock synchronization in distributed systems – a comparison

GRIN - Verlag für akademische Texte

Der GRIN Verlag mit Sitz in München hat sich seit der Gründung im Jahr 1998 auf die
Veröffentlichung akademischer Texte spezialisiert.

Die Verlagswebseite www.grin.com ist für Studenten, Hochschullehrer und andere Akade-
miker die ideale Plattform, ihre Fachtexte, Studienarbeiten, Abschlussarbeiten oder Disser-
tationen einem breiten Publikum zu präsentieren.

Dokument Nr. V69617 aus dem GRIN Verlagsprogramm

Harald Bachner

Clock synchronization in distributed systems – a comparison

GRIN Verlag

Bibliografische Information der Deutschen Nationalbibliothek: Die Deutsche Bibliothek
verzeichnet diese Publikation in der Deutschen Nationalbibliografie; detaillierte bibliografische Daten sind im Internet über http://dnb.d-nb.de/ abrufbar.

1. Auflage 2007
Copyright © 2007 GRIN Verlag
http://www.grin.com/
Druck und Bindung: Books on Demand GmbH, Norderstedt Germany
ISBN 978-3-638-67366-2

Bachelorarbeit

Clock Synchronization in Distributed Systems – A Comparison

ausgeführt von
Harald Bachner

Wien, 11. 02. 2007

Ausgeführt an der Fachhochschule Technikum Wien
Studiengang Informations- und Kommunikationssysteme

Abstract

Clock synchronization is a necessary and critical part in most distributed systems. For many years NTP was the state-of-the-art way of synchronizing computer clocks distributed in space. However, as recent advances in miniaturization lead to the construction of smaller, more powerful and less power consuming computers, embedded devices, sensors and actuators, the need for more precise time synchronization grew.

This work thus sets out to compare selected approaches to clock synchronization in distributed systems. The well known Global Positioning System is disseminating accurate time and frequency information from the International Institutes that keep the time, NTP can still do the same, but at different levels of accuracy as well as cost. Clock synchronization protocols like IEEE1588 or TTP and bus architectures like FlexRay evolved from the need to further propagate the timing information within small networks and therefore staying within the specified limits of preciseness.

Kurzfassung

Taktgeber Synchronisation ist ein notwendiger und entscheidender Teil in den meisten verteilten Systemen. Für viele Jahre war NTP die State of the Art Methode des Synchronisierens. Die Fortschritte in der Miniaturisierung, die zu immer kleineren, leistungsfähigeren und weniger Energie verbrauchenden Computern, eingebetteten Systemen, Sensoren und Aktuatoren führte, resultierte in der Notwendigkeit noch genauerer Zeitsynchronisierung.

Diese Arbeit versucht die ausgewählten Synchronisierungs-Mechanismen und Protokolle in verteilten Systemen zu vergleichen. Das weithin bekannte Global Positioning System schickt hochpräzise Zeit- und Frequenzinformationen aus, basierend auf Daten der internationalen Institute, die die Zeit „hüten". NTP kann bei geringeren Kosten dasselbe tun, erreicht aber nicht das hohe Präzisionslevel von GPS.

Synchronisierungs-Protokolle wie IEEE1588 oder TTP einerseits und Busarchitekturen wie FlexRay andererseits entwickelten sich aus der Notwendigkeit, die Zeit-Informationen innerhalb kleinerer Netze mit hoher Genauigkeit und unter Einhaltung von Präzisionsgrenzwerten zu verbreiten.

Eidesstattliche Erklärung

„Ich erkläre hiermit an Eides Statt, dass ich die vorliegende Arbeit selbstständig angefertigt habe. Die aus fremden Quellen direkt oder indirekt übernommenen Gedanken sind als solche kenntlich gemacht. Die Arbeit wurde bisher weder in gleicher noch in ähnlicher Form einer anderen Prüfungsbehörde vorgelegt und auch noch nicht veröffentlicht."

Wien, am 12. 02. 2007

Harald Bachner

Contents

1. Task Definition

Means (e.g. IEEE1588, NTP, GPS, FlexRay, TTP) to synchronize the clocks of computers in a distributed system shall be compared in this work taking the most recent literature into account. Important properties of different approaches to clock synchronization shall be highlighted and discussed. The basic principles of the clock synchronization approaches under consideration in this work shall be presented. Finally the performance and cost of the different approaches shall be contrasted.

2. Introduction

> "A man with a watch knows what time it is.
> A man with two watches is never sure".
> -- unknown.

We use clocks to synchronize ourselves with other people or procedures. How accurate the clock needs to be, depends on the circumstances: If one has to catch the train, accuracies of a couple of seconds or even a minute might be okay. Within sports milliseconds may decide who the winner is.

Modern distributed systems like measurement and automation systems, airplanes and even automobiles contain multiple networked devices and often require accurate timing in order to be able to synchronize events like coordinating distributed motion controllers and to correlate data.

Even when initially set accurately, real clocks will differ after some amount of time due to clock drift, caused by clocks counting time at slightly different rates. These clock drift rates differ over time, differ with temperature and even differ with aging of the clocks.

In a centralized system the solution to clock drift is trivial: the centralized server will dictate the system time because time is unambiguous. When a process wants to know the time, it makes a system call and the kernel tells it. If process A asks for the time, and then a little later process B asks for the time, the value that B gets will certainly be higher than the value A got (Tanenbaum / Van Steen 2002).

Situations get more difficult when changing to distributed systems where every node has its own internal clock and common agreement about time readings need to be established. Therefore synchronization of clocks, which can either be done in software, hardware or in a hybrid mixture of both, is necessary.

Clocks are checked periodically whether the inaccuracy is tolerable and are adjusted if necessary. This process is primarily done by communication between better and worse clocks. Inaccurate clocks and clocks which may not deviate that much have to be adjusted more frequently. (Weibel H., 2005)

3. Clocks, Time and Frequency

3.1. Clock Basics

Most clocks basically consist of an oscillator (a device that generates events at regular intervals), and a counting mechanism for determining the length of the second or some other desired time interval. The rate at which the oscillating events occur must be calibrated, so there must be standards set by convention or defined by some committee. (Clynch R., Allan D. et al.)

3.2. Current definition of a second of time

The unit of time, the second, was once considered to be the fraction 1/86400 of the mean solar day, however astronomical measurements showed that irregularities in the rotation of the Earth made this an unsatisfactory definition. Therefore the second was redefined at the 13th Conférence Générale des Poids et Mesures (CGPM) 1967/68 by the following: The second is the duration of 9 192 631 770 periods of the radiation corresponding to the transition between the two hyperfine levels of the ground state of the caesium 133 atom. (BIPM)

3.3. Coordinated Universal Time (UTC)

> UTC, the "Official Time for the World". (Allan D. et al., 1997)

UTC is an international agreed upon time scale, it is the ultimate standard for time-of-day, time interval and frequency (Bishop R., 2002). It is maintained by the Bureau International des Poids et Mesures (BIPM) in France. The time scale forms the basis for the coordinated dissemination of standard frequencies and time signals. The UTC scale is adjusted by the insertion of leap seconds to ensure approximate agreement with the time derived from the rotation of the Earth. These leap seconds are inserted on the advice of the International Earth Rotation and Reference Systems Service (IERS). (Allan D. et al., BIPM).

3.4. Types of Oscillators

More than 2 billion (2×10^9) quartz crystal oscillators are manufactured annually; this means they are the most common used oscillators nowadays. (Bishop R., 2002)

Typical quartz wristwatches use a quartz-crystal tuning fork with an oscillation frequency of 32,768 Hz. This number of oscillations is very convenient for usage in associated digital electronic circuit, because if this number is divided by 2^{15}, which is easy for a digital chip divider, it results in one cycle per second (Allan D. et al.).

Many different types of crystal oscillators do exist, in this thesis the focus when comparing them will be on the following only:
- XO (crystal oscillator),
- OCXO (oven-controlled crystal oscillator),

In OCXO the crystal is enclosed in a small insulated container together with a heating element and a temperature sensor. This way the crystal is kept at a constant temperature and its frequency stability is increased.
- VCXO (voltage-controlled crystal oscillator),
- TCXO (temperature-compensated crystal oscillator),
- MCXO (microcomputer-compensated crystal oscillator)

When comparing the quality of oscillators with respect to its instabilities like
- aging,
- noise,
- frequency changes with temperature,
- acceleration,
- ionizing radiation,
- power supply voltage, etc.,

the terms accuracy, stability and precision are often used (Vig R. , Bishop R.). The meanings of these terms, for a frequency source, are illustrated in Fig. 1 (Bishop R., 2002, p. 17-6).

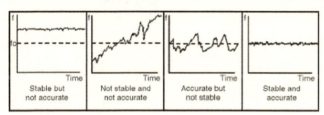

Fig. 1 The relationship between accuracy and stability. (Bishop R., 2002, p. 17-6)

Table 1 shows a comparison of salient characteristics of various selected commercial off-the-shelf (COTS) quartz oscillators according to their datasheets by Horauer M. in 2004.

	XO	VCXO	TCXO	MCXO	OCXO
Company	Quarz-Technik	AXTAL	Raltron	Temex	MTI
Type	TS-14/5	AXIS10	TX045	QEM77-AH	230-0666
Frequency stability vs. Temperature	$\pm20ppm$ -20/+70°C	$\pm15ppm$ -20/+70°C	$\pm1ppm$ -20/+70°C	$\pm20ppb$ -30/+85°C	$\pm10ppb$ -30/+70°C
Frequency stability vs. supply voltage change	$\pm2ppm$ $\pm10\%$	$\pm3ppm$	$\pm0.2ppm$ $\pm5\%$	$\pm1ppb$ $\pm5\%$	$\pm0.5ppb$
Frequency stability vs. load change		$\pm2ppm$	$\pm0.2ppm$ $\pm10\%$	$\pm1ppb$ +1 gate	$\pm0.5ppb$
Stability/1 sec.				20ppb	0.1ppb
Stability/ 1 day				1ppb	0.5ppb
Stability/ 1 month				10ppb	
Stability/ 1 year	$\pm5ppm$	$\pm3ppm$	$\pm1ppm$		70ppb
Phase Noise					
$[dBc]@1Hz$					-95
$[dBc]@10Hz$		-80	-70		-125
$[dBc]@100Hz$		-110	-100		-145
$[dBc]@1kHz$		-135	-130		-150
$[dBc]@10kHz$		-145	-140		-160
$[dBc]@100kHz$			-140		-160
Size $[cm^3]$	1.36	0.82	2.1	19.3	19
Warmup Time		4ms			5min.
Power [W]	0.225	0.25	0.1	0.03	1.4/5

Table 1 Salient characteristics of COTS Quartz Oscillators (from datasheets) (Horauer M., p. 30, 2004)

Atomic oscillators offer better long-term stability and accuracy than even the best quartz oscillators (Bishop R.). They are either based on using Rubidium or Cesium and sometimes they are even combined with other crystal oscillators like the RbXO (rubidium crystal oscillator), which consists of a crystal oscillator (for example a MCXO) which is synchronized with a built-in rubidium standard which is run only occasionally to save power.

Vig R. (as cited by Horauer M. in 2004) has done a comparison of salient characteristics of frequency standards including their accuracies, stabilities, power consumptions and prices as shown in Table 2.

	Quartz Oscillators			Atomic Oscillators		
	TCXO	MCXO	OCXO	Rubidium	RbXO	Cesium
Accuracy/year	2ppm	60ppb	10ppb	0.5ppb	0.7ppb	0.02ppb
Aging/year	0.5ppm	20ppb	5ppb	0.2ppb	0.2ppb	0
Frequency stability vs. Temperature	0.5ppm -55/+85°C	30ppb -55/+85°C	1ppb -55/+85°C	0.3ppb -55/+68°C	0.5ppb -55/+85°C	0.02ppb -28/+65°C
Stability/1 sec.	1ppb	0.3ppb	0.001ppb	0.003ppb	0.005ppb	0.05ppb
Size $[cm^2]$	10	50	20-200	800	1200	6000
Warmup Time [min]	0.1 (to 1ppm)	0.1 (to 20ppb)	4 (to 10ppb)	3 (to 0.5ppb)	3 (to 0.5ppb)	20 (to 0.02ppb)
Power [W]	0.05	0.04	0.6	20	0.65	30
Price (USD)	100	1000	2000	8000	10000	40000

Table 2 Comparison of frequency standards' salient characteristics (estimates). (Vig R. as cited by Horauer M., p. 30, 2004)

According to National Institute of Standards and Technology (NIST)[1] clock accuracies of 10^{-9} seconds per day can be maintained with atomic clocks, therefore atomic clocks are the most precise clocks on Earth (and space).

So far atomic clocks are still far too expensive and too big in size to be used in inexpensive computers. But this might change in near future, as scientists from NIST have demonstrated in 2004 that it is possible to build a chip-scaled atomic clock. According to the researchers, the clock was believed to be one hundredth the size of any other.

Fig. 2 shows the schematics of the assembly process plus a photograph of the miniature atomic clock which only has a volume of 9.5 mm^3 and dissipates less than 75 mW of power (Knappe S. et al.)

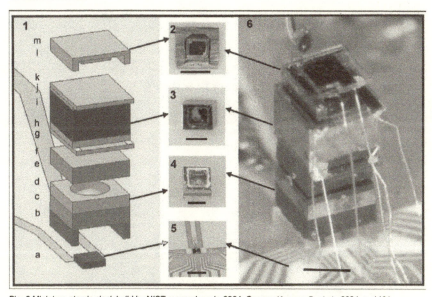

Fig. 2 Miniature atomic clock build by NIST researchers in 2004. Source: Knappe S. et al., 2004, p. 1461

3.5. Time Dissemination

Highest quality clocks are very expensive and generally used only by national time organizations, which know time very well. But they need to get it to the users, which want to synchronize their less precise clock to the time standards. Time needs to be disseminated. (Clynch R., 2002)

---

[1] http://www.nist.gov/

3.5.1. Sources of Time Synchronization Errors

Non-determinism is the main reason for time synchronization errors. For a better understanding it is helpful to characterize the sources of latencies into the following categories as done by Syed A./Heidemann J. in 2006:

- **Send Time:**

Writing a message takes time and even after writing a timestamp into a message, that message still has to travel down the protocol stack before being actually sent out at the media. Meanwhile, context switches, system calls, etc. can add some extra jitter to the amount of time needed.

- **Access Time**

That's the time spent while waiting for access to the transmission channel. In some networks collisions can occur and retransmissions might be necessary.

- **Propagation Time**

The time needed for the message to travel on the physical layer, including all the times spent in switches, hubs, routers, or other network equipment on the way, where the packet has to travel up and down the protocol stack again plus some extra time spent while packets being queued and waiting for being processed.

Packets can travel on different or asymmetric paths and these paths can have different lengths. Even a single twisted pair network cable has different cable lengths by design for each twisted pair to reduce far end cross talk (FEXT).

- **Receive Time**

The time spent within the receiver, from the network interface all the way up to the application layer.

4. Selected Clock Synchronization Protocols and Mechanisms

4.1. The IEEE Standard 1588

The idea to the **Precision Time Protocol (PTP)** was originally born at the end of the 90s of the last century at Agilent Technologies[2]. Out of the problem of creating clear time relations between measured values picked up at distributed points PTP was developed with the following goals:

- Accuracy to at least microsecond and preferably nanosecond levels.
- Minimal network, computing and hardware resource requirements hence to be applicable to low-end as well as high-end devices.
- Minimal or no systems administration needed at the nodes.

(IEEE Standard 1588-2002, Weibel H. 2005)

The methods developed at Agilent Technologies were submitted as a suggestion for standardization and passed as a standard under the name "1588 - IEEE Standard for a Precision Clock Synchronization Protocol for Networked Measurement and Control Systems" in November 2002.

According to NIST the standard 1588 is in the process of being revised and updated. Version 2 is expected to be available in spring 2007. (NIST IEEE 1588 website)

4.1.1. Operational Overview

According to the IEEE Standard 1588-2002 PTP is based on IP multicast communication and is not restricted to Ethernet. In fact, it can be used on any network technology that supports multicasting. Nevertheless, this thesis focuses furthermore on Ethernet only.

PTP scales for a large number of nodes because a master can serve many slaves with a single multicast pair of Sync and Follow_up messages.

For optimal clock synchronization performance Network delay between master and slave on a subnet must be symmetric.

The most precise clock in the network is selected automatically using the "best master clock algorithm". This clock then synchronizes all other clocks.

As seen in Fig. 3 (Weibel H. 2005) PTP's operating principle is to consecutively exchange messages to determine the offset between master and slave and also the message transit delay through the network

---

[2] http://www.agilent.com/

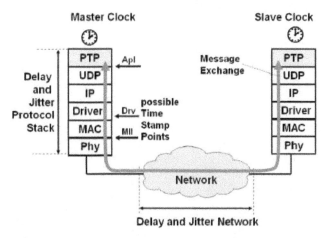

Fig. 3 PTP message exchange (Weibel H. 2005)

For calculating the offset correction, the master cyclically transmits Sync messages to the slave clock at defined intervals (by default every 2 seconds). A time stamping mechanism determines the exact transmission time **t1** as precise as possible and sends it down to the slave on behalf of a second message, the Follow_up message (see Fig. 4).

The slave clock identifies the precise reception time **t2** of the Sync message. After receiving the Sync and the corresponding Follow_up message, the slave clock calculates the offset correction in relation to the master clock.

The slave afterwards sends a Delay_Req message back to the master. After passing down the protocol stack the transmission time **t3** is noticed and compared with the timestamp **t4** which shows the masters time when receiving the Delay_Req message (before passing it up the protocol stack).

By differentiating network transfer time from the time needed to pass up or down the protocol stack the frequency drift can be compensated much more precisely.

The precision of PTP also depends on the latency created by network devices like switches, which have a load dependent packet processing time of typically 2 to 10 µs. Plus, there might be some extra time added to the transmission jitter if there are one or more long packets before the Sync packet. Even if prioritization of packets according to IEEE 802.1p is enabled extra time of up to122 µs could be needed. (IEEE Standard 1588-2002, Weibel H. 2005)

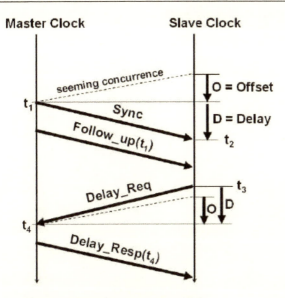

Fig. 4 Offset and Delay Measurement (Weibel H. 2005)

To solve this, so-called Boundary Clocks (see Fig. 5) are used in switches, which then act as a slave towards the master clock and act as master clock towards all the other attached slaves. Doing it this way, most internal latencies and jitters in the switch can be compensated and cause less negative influence on clock synchronization accuracy.

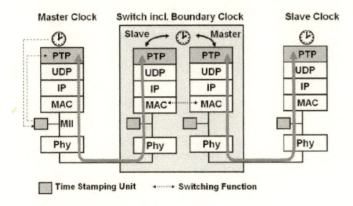

Fig. 5 Boundary Clock (Weibel H. 2005)

4.1.2. PTP Time Stamping Implementations

Clock synchronization accuracy highly depends on time stamp accuracy. Highest accuracies are obtained when implementing time stamping in hardware. When doing it in software placing the mechanism closer to the network driver gets better results than time stamping on the application layer level (Weibel H. 2005).

4.1.3. Accuracy under Real Conditions

Clock synchronization accuracies between distributed devices are in the range of +/-100 ns, or better. (Weibel H. 2005)

4.1.4. Pros and Cons

Horauer M. (2004) sees the following pros and cons when analyzing IEEE 1588:

Pros:
- Time stamping close to the physical layer is convenient and gives good results.
- PTP has the potential to become a robust, self-configuring protocol that possibly can support a multitude of different bus systems (field busses, PC-based bus-systems, etc).
- The Boundary Clock mechanism can minimize delay fluctuations introduced by switches and routers to achieve a tighter accuracy.

Cons:
- Time representation and 64-bit timestamps are not sufficient to cover granularity and rate adjustment effects as outlined in Schmid U.(1996).
- The master-slave approach outlined in PTP has several shortcomings concerning fault-tolerance.
- The delay between a SYNC message and a corresponding Follow_up packet can degrade the achievable precision due to freewheeling clocks at either side.

4.1.5. Conclusion

The PTP has further potential for higher precision. It is suited for applications which need a time synchronization of distributed clocks of highest accuracy in a limited network domain. Many manufacturers have already begun appropriate development and started evaluating their first prototypes (Weibel H. 2005).

4.2. The Network Time Protocol (NTP)

4.2.1. Technical Details

NTP is a protocol designed to synchronize the clocks of computers over a network. NTP version 3 is an internet draft standard, formalized in RFC 1305. NTP version 4 is a significant

revision of the NTP standard, and is the current development version, but has not been formalized in an RFC. Simple NTP (SNTP) version 4 is described in RFC 2030.

The goals of the NTP are to:
- Enable clients across the internet to be accurately synchronized to UTC despite message delays. Statistical techniques are used for filtering data and gauging the quality of the results.
- Provide a reliable service that can survive lengthy losses of connectivity. This means having redundant paths and redundant servers.
- Enable clients to synchronize frequently and offset the effects of clock drift.
- Provide protection against interference by authenticating data sources.

(Krzyzanowski P. (2002), RFC 1305 (Version 3))

The NTP servers are arranged into strata:
- the first stratum contains the primary servers, which are servers that have direct access to an accurate UTC time source (e.g. via GPS, see chapter 4.3).
- The second stratum contains the secondary servers. These machines are synchronized from the primary stratum servers.
- The third stratum contains tertiary servers that are synchronized from the secondary servers, and so on.

This hierarchical structure as shown in Fig. 6 by Krzyzanowski P. (2002) scales well and it has the ability to detect rogue clocks.

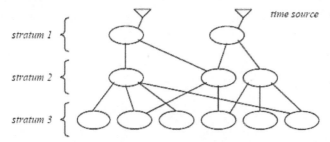

Fig. 6 hierarchical structure of NTP (Krzyzanowski P.,2002)

NTP uses a 64-bit value for the clock which offers 233 picosecond resolution.

NTP transactions occur about once per minute, when first started, increasing gradually to once per 17 minutes under common conditions (Deeths D./Brunette G., 2001).

The accuracy mainly derives from its advanced hybrid phase-lock/frequency lock loop algorithm with nearly 20 years of evolution (Gleeson M., 2004).

> "NTP may take several minutes or even hours to adjust a system's time to the ultimate degree of accuracy. There are several reasons for this. NTP averages the results of several time exchanges in order to reduce the effects of variable latency, so it may take several minutes for NTP to even reach consensus on what the average latency is. Generally this happens in about 5 minutes." (Deeths D./Brunette G., 2001)

To achieve higher accuracy, NTP can be tightly integrated into the kernel with an external stable oscillator as a time keeper. Accuracies of just a few microseconds are possible within a small LAN (Mills D. (1996) cited by Gleeson M., 2004).

As shown in Fig. 7 by Deeths D./Brunette G. (2001) NTP makes large adjustments occur quickly (which is called stepping) and small adjustments for correcting time differences of less than 128 ms occur slower over time (which is called slewing).

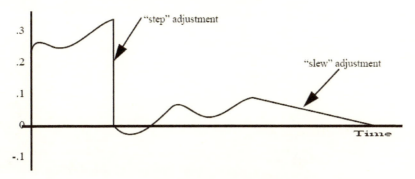

Fig. 7 Time Adjustments Using Stepping and Slewing (Deeths D./Brunette G., 2001)

4.2.2. Accuracy

It is highly advisable to take special care on choosing good quality stratum-1 servers. A survey done by Nelson Minar in December 1999 cited by ntp.org in 2007, analyzing 175,527 hosts of the NTP network, showed:
- not all NTP servers work as designed in theory.
- **Over 30% of the active stratum-1 servers had a clock error of over 10 seconds,**
- A few even had an error of more than a year.
- **Only 28% of the stratum-1 clocks found appeared to actually be useful!**

Time synchronization accuracy of a node primarily depends on network latency, which itself mainly depends on the network environment. Congested traffic could temporarily prevent synchronization, but clients can still self-adjust, based on historic drift data.

Accuracies in various environments:
- In a LAN without too many routers or other sources of network delay, synchronization within a few milliseconds is common. Anything that adds latency will of course reduce this accuracy.
- In a WAN synchronization accuracy typically ranges within 10-100 ms.
- For the Internet, synchronization accuracy is not really predictable.

(Deeths D./Brunette G.,2001, ntp.org,2007)

4.2.3. Pros and Cons

Pros:
- Inexpensive.
- Hierarchical master/slave protocol.
- Little resource overhead.
- Minimal bandwidth requirements.

- Widespread use all over the internet.

<u>Cons:</u>
- Slow adjustment in start up phase.
- Not all stratum-1 servers have the precision they should have.
- Easy to misconfigure a NTP daemon or client which would lead to poor synchronization

4.3. Clock Synchronization with the Global Positioning System[3] (GPS)

4.3.1. Technical Details

GPS is a satellite-based radio navigation system developed and operated by the U.S. Department of Defense[4].

The <u>U.S. Coast Guard Navigation Center</u> (2007) state that the GPS consists of 3 segments:

- **Space segment**

The space segment consists of a minimum of 24 operational satellites in six circular orbits 20,200 km above the earth which are spaced in orbit in a way that at any time a minimum of 6 satellites will be in view to users anywhere in the world. These satellites continuously broadcast position and time data to users throughout the world.

Each satellite carries four atomic clocks (two Cesium, two Rubidium) for timing of highest precision.

- **Control segment**

There is a master control station in Colorado Springs, with five monitor stations and three ground antennas located throughout the world. These monitors calculate the precise satellite position in orbit and analyze the offsets of the satellite's atomic clocks from UTC and adjust both if necessary.

- **User segment**

The User Segment consists of the receivers which use the GPS satellite broadcasts to compute their own precise position and velocity. Furthermore, when knowing their own position it is not difficult to calculate the distance to the satellite and adjust the time information sent out by the satellites by the time the signal needed to travel to the receiver to get very precise time information.

4.3.2. Accuracy

According to <u>Parker T./Matsakis T.</u> (2004), very-high-end GPS receivers can be calibrated to have time synchronization errors of less than 5 ns. But even the best GPS receivers can vary

---

[3] http://www.gps.gov/
[4] http://www.defenselink.mil/

by several nanoseconds over time so it is important to frequently check the calibration of GPS systems if such high accuracy is needed.

High end receivers offer accuracy better than 200 ns and cheap low-end ones are still in the range of 1 µs accuracy.

4.3.3. Deployment

For many applications it would be far too expensive, and it would also require too much extra cabling to connect every single node of the distributed system to a GPS time receiver device. Therefore in most cases only one or two GPS receivers are used to get a precise time and propagating this precise time to other nodes is done by means of other time disseminating protocols.

The following Fig. 8 shows a GPS time receiver from Galleon Systems Ltd., Birmingham, UK[5], which can deal with maximum GPS antenna cable lengths of 1,000 meter and which has a NTP server integrated for further time distribution.

Fig. 8 NTS-8000-GPS: a GPS receiver in combination with a NTP server produced by Galleon Systems Ltd., Birmingham, UK

4.3.4. Pros and Cons

Pros:
- Very high accuracy (see chapter 4.2.2).
- Possible to synchronize over very large distances.

Cons:
- High end receivers are still expensive.
- The receiver has to be in range of several satellites, therefore the use of GPS in urban areas where buildings may disguise the line of sight to the satellites may not be possible, and when GPS needs to be used indoors lots of cabling has to be done to place the antennas outside.

---

[5] http://www.galsys.co.uk/

4.4. FlexRay

FlexRay is an automotive network communications protocol under development by the FlexRay Consortium[6]. The protocol specifications are in review stage. Full use of FlexRay is expected in 2008 (FlexRay, 2007 and Wikipedia FlexRay, 2007)

4.4.1. Technical Details

All of the following technical details are based upon the FlexRay Protocol Specification Version 2.1).

4.4.1.1. Topology

FlexRay offers a wide rage of topologies:

- **Dual bus topology:** as shown in Fig. 9., where a node can be connected to either both channels A and B (nodes A, C, and E) or only to channel A (node D), or only to channel B (node B)

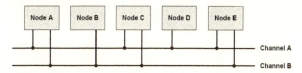

Fig. 9 Dual channel bus configuration. (FlexRay Protocol Specification Version 2.1 p. 22)

- **Single bus topology:** In this case, all nodes are connected to only one bus.
- **Active star topology:** it can be either single or dual channel (see Fig. 10). Each network channel must be free of closed rings, and there can be no more than two star couplers on a network.

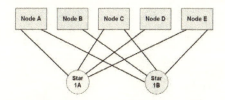

Fig. 10 Dual channel single star configuration . (FlexRay Protocol Specification Version 2.1 p. 22).

- It is also possible to have a channel configuration with **cascaded stars** (see Fig. 11)

---

[6] http://www.flexray.com/

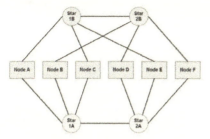

Fig. 11 Dual channel cascaded star configuration. (FlexRay Protocol Specification Version 2.1 p. 23)

4.4.1.2. Media Access

All FlexRay nodes respectively all messages are assigned to defined timeslots, in which they have the exclusive right to access the media. A static assignment of bandwidth to nodes respectively to messages via fixed timeslots wouldn't use the bandwidth efficiently.

Therefore FlexRay offers the choice of two media access schemes by dividing a recurring communication cycle into a
- **static part** with fixed timeslots, where media access is based upon a static time division multiple access (TDMA) scheme and a
- **dynamic part** with a dynamic mini-slotting based scheme. Only if there is a media access on the bus during a mini-slot interval, the timeslot can be dynamically extended. Therefore bandwidth is only used when really needed.

4.4.1.3. Bit Rates

Each channel commonly operates with 10Mbit/s (but data rates of 2.5 or 5 Mbit/s are possible as well if slower speed is required). Dual channel technology is primarily used to increase fault tolerance by redundant transmission of messages, but it is possible to send different data on both channels and therefore double the data rate.

4.4.1.4. Synchronizing the Nodes

Implementing synchronous functions and saving bandwidth by reducing the spacing between two messages, the distributed components which all have their own clocks (local time) need to establish a common time basis (global time).

Clock synchronization guarantees that time deviations amongst cluster nodes stay within the defined precision. Two types of time differences between nodes can be characterized:
- **Offset (phase) differences** and
- **Rate (frequency) differences**.

Clock synchronization consists of two simultaneous processes.
- A **macrotick generation process (MGP)**, which controls the cycle and

- The **clock synchronization process (CSP)** which is responsible for initialization at cycle start. It gauges and stores deviation values and calculates offset and rate correction values.

Fig. 12 shows the relationship between the media access schedule and the 2 processes.

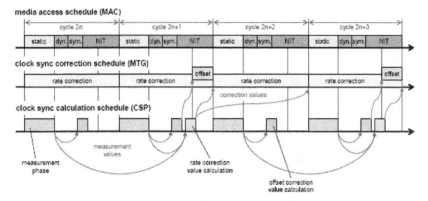

Fig. 12 Timing relationship between clock synchronization, media access schedule, and the execution of clock synchronization functions. (FlexRay Protocol Specification Version 2.1 p. 172)

4.4.1.5. Structure of FlexRay Nodes

As displayed in Fig. 13 from IXXAT Automation GmbH[7], (2007) a typical FlexRay node consists of a:

- Host processor
- FlexRay-communication-controller (CC)
- A Bus-Guardian (BG) and a
- Bus Driver (BD)

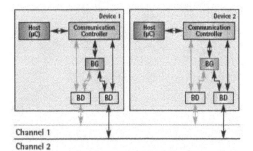

Fig. 13 FlexRay nodes (IXXAT Automation GmbH, 2007)

---

[7] http://www.ixxat.de

4.4.2. Pros and Cons

The FlexRay Protocol Specification Version 2.1 clearly shows the following:

Pros:
- Time triggered behaviour
- Redundancy
- Safety
- Fault tolerance
- Clock synchronization via a global time base
- Collision-free bus access
- Guaranteed message latency
- Message oriented addressing via identifiers
- Dynamic bandwidth allocation (per node as well as per channel)
- High data rate (10 megabits per second)

Cons:
- Doesn't scale to larger networks

4.4.3. Conclusion

FlexRay offers much more than just precise clock synchronization. It is specially designed to meet high real-time and fault tolerance requirements for usage in automobiles. (e.g. drive-by-wire)

4.5. The Time-Triggered Protocol[8] (TTP)

TTP was specifically designed to meet all the stringent requirements in connection with the implementation of fault-tolerant safety-critical high-speed applications with distributed systems.

4.5.1. Technical Details

There are 2 types of TTP:

- **The Time-Triggered Light Weight Protocol (TTP/A)**
  TTP/A is a low cost version of the TTP protocol family, which is not fault-tolerant but still has the favourable timing and time synchronisation properties. It is mainly used in field bus applications connecting nodes with sensors and actuators.

- **TTP/C**
  TTP/C is fault-tolerant and mainly used for safety-critical hard real-time applications. For example TTP is deployed within the jet engine control systems in the Lockheed Martin F-16 jet fighter airplane and in the cabin pressure control system on the Airbus A380.

---

[8] http://www.ttagroup.org/

Further analyses of TTP/A will be out of scope of this work, the focus will be on TTP/C.

TTP uses continuous communication of all connected nodes via redundant data buses at predefined intervals in the range of microseconds. It uses TDMA as media access strategy and the communication is time-triggered, which means that a node may only transmit when the current time-slot is reserved for it.

As shown in Fig. 14 by Horauer M. (2004), a typical TTP/C host has its own processor to perform the application specific tasks, below that there is a communication network interface (CNI) and adjacent to the physical layer there is a bus guardian ensuring the correct behaviour of a node by controlling the bus access of the TTP/C controller. Upon any violation of the access pattern it just terminates the controller operations.

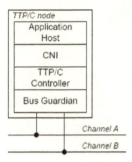

Fig. 14 TTP/C node (Horauer M., p. 41, 2004)

In a time-triggered architecture information about system behaviour is known a-priori. This knowledge is useful for reducing the overhead and for the efficient implementation of several protocol services. For example it is not necessary to carry the value of the sending time in a (synchronization) message because it is known a-priori and the time difference between the expected message arrival time and the observed receiving time indicates the clock deviation. (Horauer M.,2004)

Every node contains a local clock and clock synchronization is very similar to the FlexRay architecture, except that there is no dynamic bandwidth allocation in TTP.

4.5.2. Pros and Cons

The following pros and cons can be deduced from the TTP/C Protocol Specification Document (TTTech, 2003):

Pros:
- Fault tolerant.
- Inexpensive.
- Focus on safety-critical high-speed applications.
- High protocol efficiency.
- No data collisions.
- Various kinds of bus structure (bus, star, etc.).
- Broadcast communication possible.

- External time reference via time gateway nodes possible (which can be connected to GPS time receivers).

Cons:
- No Dynamic bandwidth allocation.
- Doesn't scale to larger networks.

5. Conclusion

In this paper various forms of time synchronization have been explored and compared. It can be concluded that some protocols are more precise than others, but this should not be the only aspect when choosing a time disseminating protocol for a distributed system. All the protocols have pros and cons and are tailored for special environments.

GPS offers much better time dissemination accuracies than NTP, at the expense of extra hardware cost, the need to place the antenna in direct view to the GPS satellites and higher power consumption.

NTP, on the other side, is normally just a piece of software running on a node and therefore it is much cheaper than GPS and IEEE1588. Time dissemination accuracies vary widely with the quality and distance of the time servers. When combining it with GPS high accuracies within a LAN can be reached.

IEEE1588 is not combating in the same field as GPS, it focuses on much smaller spatial extents, using special hardware and it therefore results in greater accuracies than NTP.

FlexRay and TTP come with their own bus-systems to meet the much more stringent safety critical requirements in their fields. In contrast to NTP and IEEE1588 they do not deal with the IP protocol. There is not always the need to sync their time closely to UTC, but if needed it can be done by placing a timeserver into the bus-system.

Table 3 follows a table from Eidson J. (2005) and shows a comparison of the protocols IEEE 1588, NTP, GPS, FlexRay and TTP.

	IEEE-1588	NTP	GPS	FlexRay	TTP
Communications	Network	Internet	Satellite	Bus or star	Bus or star
Target accuracy	Sub-microsecond	Few milliseconds	Sub-microsecond	Sub-microsecond	Sub-microsecond
Spatial extent	A few subnet	Wide area	Wide area	Local bus/star	Local bus/star
Hardware?	For highest accuracy	No	RF receiver and processor	Yes	Yes
Update interval	~2 seconds	Varies, nominally seconds	~1 second	Every TDMA cycle, ~ms	Every TDMA cycle, ~ms
Administration	Self organizing	Configured	N/A	Configured	Configured
Resources	Small network message and computation footprint	Moderate network and computation footprint	Moderate computation footprint	Moderate	Moderate
Style	Master/slave	Peer ensemble	Client/server	Distributed	Distributed

Table 3 Comparison of the Protocols

List of Figures

List of Tables

Glossary and Abbreviations

bus guardian an electronic component that protects a channel from interference caused by communication that is not temporally aligned with the cluster's communication schedule by limiting the times that a communication controller can transmit to those times allowed by the schedule.

COTS commercial off-the-shelf

FEXT Far end cross talk is an electromagnetic interference, a type of crosstalk, introduced on UTP by close-by wires, usually running in parallel with the FEXT induced wire.

FlexRay a new automotive network communications protocol under development by the FlexRay Consortium

GPS Global Positioning System

IEEE (pronounced as eye-triple-e) Institute of Electrical and Electronics Engineers

MCXO microcomputer-compensated crystal oscillator

NTP Network Time Protocol

OCXO oven-controlled crystal oscillator

PTP Precision Time Protocol, a protocol defined in IEEE1588 standard that allows precise time synchronization in networks

RbXO rubidium crystal oscillator

TCXO temperature-controlled crystal oscillator

TDMA Time division multiple access

TTP Time-Triggered Protocol

UTC Coordinated Universal Time

UTP Unshielded twisted pair cabling

XO crystal oscillator

Bibliography

Allan, D et al., 1997, The Science of Timekeeping, Hewlett Packard Application Note 1289, viewed 31 January 2007
<http://www.allanstime.com/Publications/DWA/Science_Timekeeping/>

Bishop, R., 2002. The Mechatronics Handbook, Boca Raton, CRC Press Inc

Bureau International des Poids et Mesures, 2007, SI brochure,Section 2.1.1.3, Sèvres Cedex, France, viewed 2 February 2007,
<http://www.bipm.fr/en/si/si_brochure/chapter2/2-1/second.html>

Clynch, R., 2002, Precise Time and Time Interval, Clocks, Time Frames and Frequency, Department of Oceanography, Naval Postgraduate School, Monterey, Ca 94934, viewed 31 January 2007 <http://www.gmat.unsw.edu.au/snap/gps/clynch_pdfs/pttinote.pdf>

Deeths, D./Brunette, G., 2001. Using NTP to Control and Synchronize System Clocks - Part I: Introduction to NTP. Sun BluePrints™ OnLine - July 2001. viewed 12 January 2007
<http://www.sun.com/blueprints/0701/NTP.pdf>

Eidson, J. 2005.IEEE-1588 Standard for a Precision Clock Synchronization Protocol for Networked Measurement and Control Systems -A Tutorial-. Agilent Technologies. viewed 30 January 2007 http://ieee1588.nist.gov/tutorial-basic.pdf

Elson, J. et al., 2002, Fine-Grained Network Time Synchronization using Reference Broadcasts, University of California, Los Angeles, viewed 5 February 2007,
<http://lecs.cs.ucla.edu/Publications/papers/broadcast-osdi.pdf>

FlexRay Communications System Protocol Specification Version 2.1, 2005. viewed 1 January 2007 <http://www.FlexRay.com/>

FlexRay Consortium, 2007,Website viewed 18 January 2007 <http://www.FlexRay.com/>

Gleeson   M., 2004. A Real Time Implementation of TBMAC using IEEE 802.11b. Dissertation. University of Dublin, Trinity College. viewed 18 January 2007
<https://www.cs.tcd.ie/publications/tech-reports/reports.05/TCD-CS-2005-10.pdf>

HORAUER, M., 2004. CLOCK SYNCHRONIZATION IN DISTRIBUTED SYSTEMS. Clock Synchronization in Distributed Systems, Dissertation,Technischen Universität Wien

IEEE Standard 1588™-2002, 2002. IEEE Standard for a precision Clock Synchronization Protocol for Networked Measurement and Control Systems

Knappe S. et al., 2004. A microfabricated atomic clock, Appl. Phys. Lett., Vol. 85, No. 9, 30 August 2004, viewed 17 January 2007 <http://tf.nist.gov/general/pdf/1945.pdf>

Krzyzanowski P., 2002. Clock Synchronization. Rutgers University – CS 417: Distributed Systems, viewed 31 January 2007
<http://www.cs.rutgers.edu/~pxk/rutgers/notes/pdf/06-clocks.pdf>

Maróti, M. et al, 2004, The Flooding Time Synchronization Protocol, Nashville, USA, viewed 5 February 2007,
<http://www.isis.vanderbilt.edu/publications/archive/Maroti_M_11_3_2004_The_Floodi.pdf>

Mills D., 1992. RFC1305: Network Time Protocol (version 3).

Mills D., 1996. RFC2030: Simple Network Time Protocol (version 4).

Mills, D., 1996.. The network computer as precision timekeeper. In Proceedings of Precision Time and Time Interval (PTTI) Applications and Planning Meeting (Dec 1996), pp. 96–108.

Minar N., 1999. A Survey of the NTP Network. viewed 18 January 2007 <http://alumni.media.mit.edu/~nelson/research/ntp-survey99>

National Institute of Standards and Technology, IEEE 1588 Website, 2007. viewed 17 January 2007 <http://ieee1588.nist.gov/>

ntp.org, 2007. The NTP FAQ and HOWTO. Website, viewed 18 January 2007 <http://www.ntp.org/ntpfaq/NTP-a-faq.htm>

Parker T./Matsakis T, 2004 Time and Frequency Dissemination: Advances in GPS Transfer Techniques, GPS World, pp. 32-38, viewed 2 January 2007 <http://tf.nist.gov/general/pdf/1998.pdf>

SCHMID, U. 1996. Interval-based Clock Synchronization. In Seminar-Report of Dagstuhl-Seminar on Time Services (Schloß Dagstuhl, Germany, Mar. 1996), p. 7.

Syed A./Heidemann, J., 2006, Time Synchronization for High Latency Acoustic Networks. In Proceedings of the IEEE Infocom, Barcelona, Spain, viewed 5 February 2007, <http://www-scf.usc.edu/~asyed/papers/tshl.pdf>

Tanenbaum A./Van Steen M., 2002. Distributed Systems. Principles and Paradigms. Upper Saddle River, New Jersey: Prentice Hall International

TTTech, 2003, Time-Triggered Protocol TTP/C High-Level Specification Document Protocol Version 1.1, Vienna, Austria

U.S. Coast Guard Navigation Center, 2007. Website, viewed 27 January 2007 <http://www.navcen.uscg.gov/faq/gpsfaq.htm>

Vig, R., 1992, Introduction to Quartz Frequency Standards, Fort Monmouth, USA, viewed 3 February 2007, <http://www.ieee-uffc.org/freqcontrol/quartz/vig/vigtoc.htm>

Weibel H., 2004. Uhren mit IEEE 1588 synchronisieren, in SEV/AES 17/04, viewed 17 January 2007 < http://ines.zhwin.ch/uploads/media/Fachartikel_IEEE1588_02.pdf>

Weibel H., 2005. High Precision Clock Synchronization according to IEEE 1588 Implementation and Performance Issues, viewed 18 January 2007 <http://ines.zhwin.ch/uploads/media/embedded_World_05_Contribution_final_02.pdf>

Dokument Nr. V69617
http://www.grin.com/
ISBN 978-3-638-67366-2